Days of the

Monday

Tuesday

Wednesday

Thursday

Friday

Saturday

Sunday

Monday

I am at school.

I am reading a book.

I can see five red leaves,

four yellow leaves,

and three green leaves.

We are looking for red leaves,
and yellow leaves,
and green leaves.

Tuesday

I am at school today.

I am playing

with the big blocks.

My long road

goes under the table.

Wednesday

I am at school today.

I am making a pattern.

The pattern goes red, yellow, blue, red, yellow, blue.

Thursday

I am at school today.

Look at all the shapes!

I made a house

and a tree.

Friday

I am at school today.

I am playing with the water.

The water goes down

into this bottle.

Saturday

I am **not** at school today.

I am going shopping
with Dad.

One ice cream cone is for Dad,
and one ice cream cone is
for me.

Sunday

I am **not** at school today.

I am going to the park

with Mom and Dad.

I go to school
on Monday, Tuesday,
Wednesday, Thursday,
and Friday.

I do **not** go to school
on Saturday and Sunday.